BRITAIN IN OLD PHOTOGRAPHS

The
West Wight

Donald A. Parr

SUTTON PUBLISHING LIMITED

Sutton Publishing Limited
Phoenix Mill · Thrupp · Stroud
Gloucestershire · GL5 2BU

First published 1996

Cover photographs: (front) Walter Burnett and
his wife, and Miss Alice Burnett, Totland,
c. 1900; (back) a wedding group in Freshwater,
1887.
Title page photograph: Pining's Corner, High
Street, Yarmouth, 1881.

British Library Cataloguing in Publication Data
A catalogue record for this book is available from the
British Library.

ISBN 0-7509-1305-3

Typeset in 10/12 Perpetua.
Typesetting and origination by
Sutton Publishing Limited.
Printed in Great Britain by
Ebenezer Baylis, Worcester.

This picture of North Court, Shorwell, is believed to have been taken in 1890.

CONTENTS

After taking delivery of stores the keepers of the Needles lighthouse give a cheery wave before returning to their ever watchful vigil.

INTRODUCTION

This is the sixth book about the Isle of Wight in the Britain in Old Photographs series. The West Wight, by virtue of the use of the definite article, is something of a colloquialism but it is used here to describe the whole area of the western part of the Island. The previous five volumes in this series are concerned with the well-populated parts of the Island, but the West Wight is mainly dedicated to agriculture and the sea, and therefore consists of small villages and hamlets rather than towns. The only official town is Yarmouth, one of the smallest towns in the British Isles and also the main port of entry into the West Wight, with regular shipping traffic from Lymington in the New Forest. Neighbouring Freshwater is by far the largest centre of population in the area but it is not officially a town. It has even been described as one of the largest villages in the British Isles. So the West Wight provides a great contrast to the rest of the Island.

This contrast also applies regarding our summer visitors. Some people prefer the entertainment and bustle of the main resorts, with their theatres, sports facilities and larger hotels. Most of these are situated on the eastern side of the Island. For a couple of weeks in each year Cowes is a Mecca for the yachtsman, but through all this the West Wight remains by far the quietest area. Those who prefer the rolling downs, affording some of the best views in the south, the peace of the countryside and even the sometimes angry moods of the sea, especially around the Needles rocks at Alum Bay, visit this part of our Island year after year.

In addition to the general views, I have endeavoured within these pages to include a cross-section of village life, a task made a little easier by the fact that West Wight families have tended to remain rather more static, the farms and businesses having been handed down from father to son through the generations. Most of them are still going strong. I also thought it was important to devote quite a large section to the work of the lifeboats over the last century and the often extreme and sometimes ultimate bravery of the men who manned them. The beauty and scenery of this tranquil area which has frequently been described as 'a little Britain in miniature' is nature at her best. Unfortunately the coastal waters of the Solent and around the Needles are among the most treacherous in the country, and often witness nature at her worst. Our lifeboats, classed as 'all weather self-righting boats', frequently put to sea in gale- and hurricane-force winds, coping with heavy swells and waves of anything between 30 and 70 ft high, especially around and to the west of the Needles.

The West Wight has also been home to many celebrities over the years, mainly writers, actors and musicians. Alfred Lord Tennyson, Alfred Noyes and J.B. Priestley were some of the literary men who lived and died here. More recently, John and Mary Mills and their daughters Juliet and Hayley, Vincent Price and the late Roy Castle have enjoyed the peace of the West Wight. Musicians and conductors, such as the late Mantovani, have also lived here.

Yarmouth boasts a fine yachting association and club, and its harbour, a popular marina, is a centre both for those who like 'messing about in boats' and for those who take the sport much more seriously.

In conclusion, when our visitors have, reluctantly in most cases, returned to their own homes after their holidays, the West Wight's residents are able to have the downs and beaches, woodlands and mudflats, with their abundant bird life, to themselves once again. The glories of autumn on the Island are perfectly captured by Lawrence Wilson in his book *Portrait of the Isle of Wight*, published by Robert Hale in 1965: 'The village postman cycles past with his half empty bag. There is not a footmark on the seashore and the only sounds are the cry of gulls and the steady breathing of the sea. Then it is that you feel a sense of freedom so seldom experienced in many other places and you remember the Island's coat of arms. A triple castle between three anchors on an azure field, supported by a horse and a sea-horse, the shield resting on a green argent-coasted island lapped by an azure sea and underneath the motto: "All This Beauty is of God".'

Donald A. Parr
Totland Bay, September 1996

For many years Colwell Bay boasted an inn called the Drum and Monkey but in 1869, in honour of the late Admiral Lord Horatio Nelson, its name was changed to the Nelson. Whether this name was popular or not is hard to say, but ten years later the name was again changed to the present Colwell Bay Inn.

AROUND THE WEST WIGHT

*Enjoying the delights obtainable from Gillings bakery and
restaurant in Totland Bay, c. 1930.*

Jane Conway (extreme right), the founder of the Conway enterprises at Colwell Bay, photographed in 1921. Looking through the window is Lily Rose Conway.

Conways' boathouse, 1934.

By 1956 the Conway enterprises included not only a putting green, but boats, floats, deck chairs and beach huts as well as tea rooms. It had all started through Jane's early efforts.

Ernest Edward Conway with his boats at Colwell in 1962.

Bill Meaning serving children with ice creams at Colwell Bay, 1920.

The Conway family at their home, Middleton Cottage in Totland, in the late 1880s.

Brighstone Mill was one of a chain of water mills across the Island. With the advent of modern milling processes many of them sadly became redundant. This mill was taken over by the Fisk family of Chilton Farm who used it for the preparation of their cattle feed. It was sold in the 1980s and although the mill itself is retained, four picturesque houses have been built on the site.

Brooke Hill House stands about a mile inland but nevertheless was bought by author J.B. Priestley for its magnificent sea views. On his death in 1984 the house was converted into flats.

A delivery dray outside the cellars of the Five Bells in Brighstone in 1913. This establishment was closed in 1915 and is now the village store.

Brighstone old village, showing the New Inn, now the Three Bishops. The name was changed in the late 1970s when the brewery asked local people for suggestions. Over the years three men from the village had been ordained bishops, hence the new name. On the extreme right is the site of Wilberforce Hall.

The imposing gatehouse of Westover House at Calbourne, 1920s. This photograph shows rural Isle of Wight at its best.

Totland Chalet Hotel, 1920. This was used as a hospital during the Second World War and demolished in the late 1960s, together with the popular Lanes Inn.

Until the advent of mass tourism Brighstone village retained a charm unique to the small rural communities. Above: a horse and trap passing St Mary's parish church. Below: one of the first delivery vans in the same area some years later, in about 1925.

The Newport to Yarmouth road as it approaches Yarmouth Common, 1909. The landscape is entirely different today.

Old Yarmouth police station before it was given a 'face-lift' in the mid-1960s, resulting in the present modern-looking building with car parking space.

Totland war memorial, *c.* 1920. It was built on a butt of land that was formerly Anderson's kitchen garden.

Freshwater old mill was burned down in the 1840s and the stone from it was used in part of the construction of Stonewind Farm. Another mill was built near Windmill Lane, opposite the Conservative Club, but did not last long owing to the lack of wind caused by the surrounding buildings.

Colwell Beach, probably photographed in the early to mid-1940s. The scene retains the charm of the 1920s with the old bathing machines still to be seen.

During the 1920s and '30s, Algar and Meanings were noted for their ice cream vending. Bill Meaning serves children with ice cream in Granville Road, Totland.

These two pictures show the early development of Yarmouth waterfront. Right: the seaward side of Yarmouth Quay, with the Causeway in the background. Below: looking seaward from the quay; the Wight Link car ferry terminal now occupies this area.

The Needles battery at Alum Bay was equipped with 9.2 in guns for sea defences. Above: the guns being unloaded at Colwell Beach after their short sea crossing from Portland in 1905. Below: the guns passing along The Broadway, Totland, on their way to be installed at Alum Bay.

The original entrance to Yarmouth Castle, *c.* 1900. This entrance is still in existence, although it is no longer used and is now sited in the gardens of the George Hotel.

Calbourne village pump, 1904. At one time this was the main source of water for those living in the village. It is situated at the junction of Lynch Lane and School Lane.

The High Down Inn, Totland, 1960s. This has always been popular among locals and visitors alike. It looks much the same today.

Conways' original boathouse at Colwell Bay in the late 1920s. Bathing huts were still very much in evidence.

Totland Chalet Hotel, 1920s. At this time the hotel, beach, pier and the turf walk were all owned by one person, who discouraged the general public from even visiting the beach, thus preserving the 1920s character which still holds good today.

The original Needles Hotel at Alum Bay, which was destroyed by fire in 1910. The foundations were lost to the sea in a later landslide.

Weston Manor, the property of the Ward family, was leased first to a Spanish nursing order of nuns who cared for wayward girls. In 1962 the lease was taken over by brothers of the Dominican order known as the Order of Preachers to give residential help to men with learning difficulties. It is still being used for this purpose to this day.

Wadham's shop in Avenue Road, Freshwater, 1938. The shop closed in the early 1940s.

Freshwater village, 1890s. One may be forgiven for confusing it with a scene from an old western movie!

This very old photograph, taken from a glass plate negative, shows the Causeway linking Yarmouth town with what is now known as Hallett Chute, just before the building of the first bridge in 1858.

With the advent of the Second World War, the owners of North Court, Shorwell, turned much of their picturesque grounds into vegetable plots, as they had done during the First World War. By 1942, when this photograph was taken, the North Court residents had taken the words of the agricultural minister to heart and were digging for victory. Although the brave and gallant men of the merchant fleet daily risked their lives to keep the supply lines open, the country still relied heavily on those people who could grow their own food and those who could help to supply people in urban areas. This house at Shorwell, originally the Manor of Northschorewell, had been devised to Lacock Abbey by Amicia, widow of Baldwin de Redvers, but with the Dissolution of the Monasteries the estate came into the possession of

the Leighs. Sir John Leigh built North Court's principal wing in 1615. An interesting quotation from *Wight: Biography of an Island*, by Paul Hyland (Victor Gollancz, 1984) reads: 'Twenty years ago, the kitchen, where cooks had concocted delicacies for the likes of Count Waldstein, was a near-cubicle underground chamber seventeen feet high; it had satisfied soldiers' appetites in 1940, when North Court was the headquarters of the 2nd Battalion, The Royal Fusiliers, which manned posts between St Catherine's Point and The Needles. Now, in spacious seclusion a swimming pool heats in the sun and a spring still issues softly from its source in a flint-built shelter; it is hard even to imagine the thunder of air raids, although a 500 lb bomb fell opposite the Crown Inn, just missing St Peter's Church, and a German air crew suffered North Court's hospitality.'

Many illustrious literary people either visited or lived on the Island. The poet Algernon Swinburne made many visits in the 1890s and composed many of his poems in the library at North Court, Shorwell.

The owners of North Court allowed it to be used as the venue for many events during the period between the wars and again after 1945. This is believed to be a Red Cross fête in the 1960s.

During the First World War, families at home tried to do their bit to help the war effort. Here Edith Earl is tending the large kitchen garden at North Court in 1918.

Yarmouth Square, 1904. Little seems to have changed except the mode of transport and the addition of the dreaded yellow lines.

Before the days of refrigerators, most large houses would have ice houses or storage cellars in the garden where perishable goods could be kept cool during the summer months. Pictured here are two such structures which were built at Weston Manor in 1869. Now renovated and fitted with doors they are once again useful storage areas.

Loading flour at Gatcombe Mill, 1905. This mill, like so many others, closed with the advent of the powered mill.

Moa Place, Freshwater, c. 1900. A few years later a New Zealand family purchased the whole area and began to develop it. The first houses were built on the corner and still retain their original names, such as Hokitika and Wancanui. These houses were to be followed shortly after by the building of Moa Place in 1896. (The name Moa is derived from the now extinct flightless bird from New Zealand.)

The Westdown at Totland, looking east towards Freshwater Bay. This high point was the site of the old Nodes Beacon.

Hatherwood Point and Headon Hill. This was the site of the Hatherwood Point battery, built in 1862.

Headon Hill, looking over Hatherwood Point to the Needles. The much eroded north surface of the chalk deposits of the Headon and Osborne Bays was a sub-tropical lagoon at the time of the dinosaurs, remains of which have been found nearby at Chale.

Colwell Bay, 1940s. This is considered by some to be one of the best bathing beaches on the Island.

In its heyday Totland boasted a grand pier and the imposing Totland Bay Chalet Hotel. Unfortunately the pier now stands in a state of disrepair while the Chalet Hotel was demolished in the 1960s to make way for a housing development.

Turf Walk, Totland Bay, *c.* 1900. Totland Chalet Hotel is in the background.

Lanes Inn, 1947. The inn was incorporated within and adjacent to the Chalet Hotel and was a popular local stopping place for the purchase of both alcoholic beverages and teas.

The Royal Standard Hotel in The Avenue, Freshwater, was consumed by fire on 9 September 1905. It was later rebuilt and is still a popular hotel and pub.

These two scenes depict agricultural life at Limmerstone Farm in the 1900s. Three generations of the Downer family are among the people pictured in these photographs. Above: threshing with the aid of a steam engine. Below: shearing with hand clippers, a slow and laborious task.

Brighstone Rectory, photographed after the Second World War, when the incumbent was Revd Ralph Charlton.

An engraving of Farringford House, Freshwater, before it was purchased by Alfred Lord Tennyson.

Mrs Elsie Elizabeth Trevanion and guests at Windmill Farm, Totland, *c.* 1935.

Sheepwash Cottage, Middleton, Freshwater. This cottage stands on the site of a sixteenth-century barn. At one time the farmer's living accommodation was in the upper storey of the barn but as time passed a farmhouse and cottages for the workers were built.

The main street at Brighstone, 1909. Note the delivery van stopped on the 'wrong' side of the road – in those days they did need to worry about traffic on this still un-made thoroughfare.

To the rear of the Farringford Hotel in Bedbury Lane, Freshwater Bay, runs a pathway with a rustic bridge; this was a favourite walk of Lord Tennyson.

Farringford House, Freshwater Bay, was leased from the Seymour family by Alfred Lord Tennyson, the Poet Laureate, on a three year lease at £2.00 weekly, and with an option to purchase which he eventually did. Tennyson's own description of the house was 'Like blank verse which suited the humblest of cottages and the grandest cathedral'. Some time after his death in 1892, the house was sold. Today, it is a thriving

hotel, which is also home to the Tennyson society. These four photographs were taken at various times and usually captioned 'Farringford — seat of Lord Tennyson'. We know that the poet and his wife were keen on the new photographic apparatus and were admirers of Julia Margaret Cameron, an early photographer who lived at Dimbola in Freshwater Bay.

This monument stands on the site where Guglielmo Marconi established his first coastal wireless station in 1897. Marconi's exciting experiments attracted worldwide attention and are described on the sides of the monument. Mr Garlick, the first owner of Totland Bay sub-post office, was approached by Marconi who asked him for assistance with his first experiments at Alum Bay. A plaque on the wall outside the post office in the Broadway, Totland Bay, proudly relates their achievements.

Totland's first sub-postmaster, J.B. Garlick, pictured with his family and staff in 1902.

SECTION TWO

THE PEOPLE

Walter Burnett and his wife outside their house, Hurst View in Totland, c. 1900. The third person is believed to be Miss Alice Burnett.

Mr Ernest Walker of Freshwater, seen here on 9 September 1899, pointing into the stone grave he unearthed in a field opposite Sheepwash Farm, Totland. The grave contained a skull and an urn.

Ernest Walker showing HRH Princess Beatrice and her party the sarcophagus which he discovered in 1899. This photograph and the previous one are believed to have been taken by Robert Lever.

Members of the Freshwater and Totland Conservative Association pose for the camera during the presentation of an illuminated address to Squire Edmund Granville-Ward at Weston Manor. The men are A.W. Ellender of Seafield; Mr Bannister, Oakfield nurseryman; Frank Osborne, outfitter; Police Constable Toomer; Squire Edmund Granville-Ward, JP; Major Pakenham of Headon Hall; Mr Godsel of Granville Corner Restaurant; Robert M. Howe of Sunnyside, greengrocer and parish councillor; Mr Paul, builder; William Waterhouse, Totland Bay estate agent; and Henry Dowty of the Brickworks, The Avenue. Unfortunately this photograph is undated.

The children of the Weeks family at Calbourne, *c.* 1900. Top, from left to right: Dorothy Muriel, Edith Elizabeth, Madelaine Kate. Below left: Arthur Duncan, Wilfred Herbert, Reginald George. Below right: Ronald Frederick, Barbara Kathleen, Isobel Royal.

This early but undated photograph shows the families of William Waterhouse and Mr Adams. 'Granny' Adams (with posy) and her husband (with beard) are seated in the centre.

A wedding group in Freshwater, 1887. Note the gaily decorated hats — certainly not the head wear for high winds.

The Baker family at the Wellow Baptist Church, 1918. Back row, left to right: Fred, Alice, George. Front row: Edith, Emily, Eva, Margaret. The Baker family all made their homes in or around the village of Newbridge except for Edith, who, on attaining the age of 21, left the Island to take a position of housekeeper to a Bournemouth vicar. On the outbreak of hostilities in 1939 Edith resigned her post and joined the RAF as a cook, a post she held until 1949. After demobilization, fearing that Island life would be too quiet, she joined the Royal Mail Line as a stewardess. Her first boat was the *Astunia*, which carried troops to Korea. Then she moved on to the *Alcantara*. In all, Edith made thirteen trips to Australia before joining the renowned liner *Andes*, cruising to Argentina. Edith finally came ashore in 1969 and became a companion to a lady in Surrey. She eventually returned home to Newbridge in 1984.

The Baker family, photographed outside the schoolroom on the occasion of the wedding of Fred and Minnie at Wellow Baptist Chapel in 1928. Back row, left to right: Edith, Alice, George, Fred, Olive, Marjorie. Front row: William (father), Emily (mother), Eva.

Beltins Masonic Lodge, 1952. Among those included are Mr Harrison, Mr White, Mr Martin and Joe 'Sweeney' Todd.

Charles and Ernest Edward Conway outside their boathouse at Colwell Bay in the early 1950s.

Mrs Stanton was a well-known Yarmouth resident who worked hard for various charitable organizations. Here she is seen in a Victorian bath chair, pulled by another popular Yarmouth resident, Les Turner.

This photograph is believed to have been taken at Frank McClean's wedding. The bride's name is not recorded but the wedding was attended by Mr Adams and Mrs ('Granny') Adams. Also included in the photograph are Peggy Adams, W.J. Waterhouse, Mrs Waterhouse, Mr Meader and Miss Adams.

Lanes Inn was the venue for many parties. Some of those present at this gathering are Eric Westhorpe, Diana and Les Groves, Frank McClean, Charles Merwood, Sid Greer, Mr Palmer of The Highdown and Ron Seymour. The photograph is captioned 'Liberation Day'.

William Critchell and staff at the blacksmith's premises of Critchell & Vincent at Newbridge in 1929.

William Critchell at work on a cartwheel hub, 1930. He is chiselling the elm nave to receive the feet of the oak spokes. These are set alternately, one forward and one backward, to help spread the load.

William Critchell and staff outside the forge at Critchell & Vincent, Newbridge, 1928.

Joe Morris, the gardener at Brighstone Rectory, drinking from one of the flagons found by local builders J.R. Buckett, who were renovating his cottage at Brook in 1958.

Nellie Waterhouse of Seaview Cottage, Totland, *c.* 1903.

Mrs Adams, known to many as 'Granny' Adams, pictured outside her house in Granville Road. The house is now the Granville Stores.

Doris White, secretary of the United Reformed Church at Guyers Road in Freshwater, pictured in 1977. Doris was also a well-known member of the Hurst Hill Choir.

The Hurst Hill Choir after a concert at Chale in 1973. Included are Ernest White, Jack Robinson, Cliff Daniels, George Abey, Ron Hurst, Fred Lawrence, Daisy Jephcott, Anne Maine, Pat Payne, Stephanie Robinson, Doris White, 'Barney' Barnes, Mabel Rollison and Karen Hardy.

Wearing his life-jacket, crew member Ernest Edward Conway waits for the launch of the *Robert Flemming*, the Totland Bay lifeboat, in 1919.

Captain F. Burnett with his wife Marian at Hurst View, Totland Bay, during the Second World War.

Jacob Cotton served as a member of the lifeboat crew stationed at Totland Bay for many years.

For most of his working life Percy Guy proudly wore the uniform of the Automobile Association. He was known for his generosity to motorists and would often wave down speeding cars to warn the drivers of a police speed trap ahead.

The Needles Masonic Lodge officers for 1908/9. Back row, left to right: H.C. Simmonds, H. Marfleet, H.C. Hill. Second row: T. Hobbs, W.R. Hall, J.W. Newman, F. Fewster, W.J. Waterhouse, R. Barry. Front row: J.H. Chantry, F.W. Simmonds, C. White, H.S. St John, D. Chart, W.C. Downer.

An undated group from the Needles Masonic Lodge. Included are Captain Clarke, Mr Pink, Mr Stark, Frank McClean, Dr Kelly and Captain Hall.

An undated photograph of the Needles Masonic Lodge taken at their headquarters, Avenue House, Freshwater. Included are M. Richards, Mr Mason, Harry Barnes, Mr McManus, J.B. Garlick, W.J. Waterhouse and Frank McClean.

The Needles Masonic Lodge photographed outside their former assembly rooms at Avenue House, Freshwater, November 1927. Included are Bob Astell, Mr Peskett (vet), Mr McManus, Stan Burton, J. Newman (stonemason), Jack Hackett, Harry Barnes, Revd Mr Pratt, Sergeant-Major Arnold, J.B. Garlick, J. Fletcher, Mr Perry, D. Chart, W.J. Waterhouse, G. Cleary, Mr Kebble, Harry Milne, George Thearle, Mr Barnard, Frank McClean, Jack Downey, Mr Richards, Mr Mason, Captain Hall, Major Clark, A. Tanner, Bob Rae and Jack Starke.

Mrs Phoebe Raddings of Yarmouth. Though profoundly deaf from childhood, Phoebe rose to the rank of Honorary Commissioner of Cubs for the Isle of Wight.

In 1937 Weston Manor was leased by an order of Spanish nuns who ran it as a haven for refugees from the Spanish Civil War, and subsequently for the residential care of wayward women.

In the early 1900s gangs of workmen used to travel around the south of England with their steam traction and agricultural engines to carry out tasks that required the power of such new-fangled machines. This is the joint workforce of Geo. Ford & Sons and W. Aldridge (both mainland firms), working on the Calbourne side of Parkhurst forest in 1909. Once the trees had been felled, a steam saw was used to cut the timber into planks on the site. The steam engine these workers were using can now be seen at the Calbourne Mill Museum.

William Critchell, blacksmith, wheelwright and now undertaker! Here he is leading the cortège of John Rayner through Shalfleet in January 1929. Normally, the deceased would have been carried to the church in his coffin, but John Rayner had requested that his last journey should be made in a farm wagon.

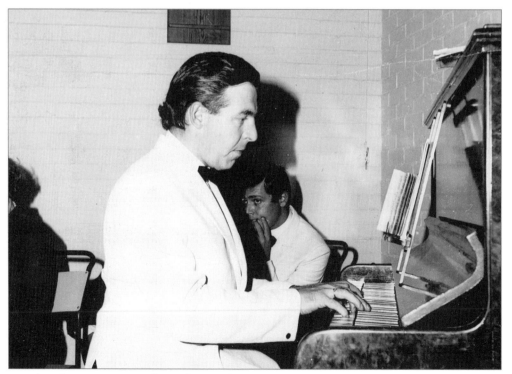

Seated at the piano, Peter White rehearses for an Armistice Day service at Brook in 1962. In the background, seated, is BBC announcer Barry Bethell.

PLACES OF WORSHIP

*The Baptist Church at Colwell was built in 1834 and has
been in continuous use ever since.*

The thatched church of St Agnus at Freshwater Bay incorporates a 1694 date stone, misleading many people into thinking that this church is more than three hundred years old. In fact it was built in 1908 from stone salvaged from an old derelict farmhouse.

St Saviour's Roman Catholic Church at Hurst Hill, Totland Bay. Before it was built in 1924, the only place of Catholic worship was the chapel at Weston Manor. It is interesting that those attending Weston Manor Chapel had also opened their own school before St Saviour's was built.

St Saviour's Chapel, Weston Manor, Totland, 1910. Built into Weston Manor, this was used as the private chapel of the Ward family who owned the Manor.

Revd Harvey Gridon, Rector of Brighstone from
1934 to 1945.

Revd Ernest Silver, Rector of Brighstone from
1908 to 1934.

Revd Ralph Charlton, Rector of Brighstone from
1945 to 1972.

Revd Gordon Broome, Rector of Brighstone from
1972 to 1980.

In the churchyard of St Saviour's at Hurst Hill, Totland Bay, stands this large monument over the Ward family grave. Although primarily from the Cowes area, the Wards also owned Weston Manor and regularly worshipped in their private St Saviour's Chapel. After the manor was leased they were still regular worshippers at the new St Saviour's Church. Some of the names on the monument include Wilfred John Ward, 1931–93, Herbert Joseph Ward, 1894–1967, and his wife Magdelen Theresa, 1888–1974. The Ward family grave is next to those of the poet Alfred Noyes (d. 1958), and his wife Mary Angela (d. 1976).

This is the funeral of a 21-year-old Gunner of the 5th Howitzer Brigade RA, which took place at Freshwater parish church in 1928. He was killed in Newport after being run down by his gun when the team of horses pulling it bolted.

The Scouts pay homage to the captain of the *Prim* which foundered on the rocks. His funeral took place at Brighstone Church on 27 February 1912.

The arrival of the cortège escorting the body of the *Prim*'s captain at the churchyard.

This is the funeral of three young children of George and Marie Salter who were caught by the tide when out winkling and drowned at Chilton on 5 April 1913. The mourners include George Baker (undertaker), John Cotton, Fred Merwood, Arthur Shotter and Harry Downer (farmer). The children who died were Ethel May, aged 10, Albert James, aged 9, and Florence Vera, aged 7.

The Methodist Church in Avenue Road, Freshwater, just before completion in 1906. It took two years to build.

Ever since its dedication the church has enjoyed a thriving congregation. As this 1996 photograph shows, the brickwork still looks as good today as it did on the day of its opening.

After the Spanish nuns had moved on, the Ward family leased Weston Manor to the Dominican Brothers of the Order of Preachers to be used for the residential care of men with learning difficulties. The brothers are pictured here in 1965. Standing, left to right: Brothers Michael, Thomas, Dory, Stephen, Sister Mary Luke, Brother Bernard. Seated is Fr (Henry) St. John.

The staff of Weston Manor, 4 October 1968. Standing, left to right: Brothers Francis, Andrew, Sister Claire, Brother Bernard. Seated: Brother Dominic, Fr Matthew (chaplain), Sister Mary Luke, Brother Michael.

Rural Shalfleet. The steeple of the church of St Michael and All Angels can be seen in the background. This church was dedicated just before the writing of the Domesday Book in 1087. In the thirteenth century, money for its upkeep was in short supply and a simple rhyme from that time runs. 'Shalfleet poor and simple people sold their bell to buy a steeple'. The bell survived and is now in Thorley church, but unfortunately the steeple did not!

Presentation to Father O'Callaghan on the occasion of his leaving St Saviour's RC Church, Hurst Hill, Totland Bay, for Australia in 1960. Left to right: Violet Higson, Father O'Callaghan, Mr Runyard.

Monsignor Gudgion in procession at St Saviour's RC Church, Hurst Hill, Totland Bay, 1937.

Brighstone Church choir, 1928. Included are W. Higgins, Mr and Mrs J. Creeth, Ernie Cooper, Bert Craven, Harry Chessil, Roland Downer, Jack Whitewood, Mr and Mrs L. Hookey, Arthur Tharle, Julia Bennett, Charlotte Mullett (in wicker chair), Miss Williams, John Mearman, Revd Ernest Silver (rector), Miss Willoughby, Wyn Cooper, Rose Snow, Marjorie and Raymond Chessil, and Stanley Maskell.

The May Day celebrations at St Saviour's Church, Hurst Hill, Totland Bay. Above: the May Queen, Monica Cluderay, with her attendants. Also included in the picture are Ann Vickers, Pat Oakham, Patrica Hall, Joan Gobey, Deanne Manuel and Alan Gobey. Below: helping with this May Day procession in the 1950s are Charlie Croad, Bill Runyard and Michael Condon.

THE YOUTH

Cub Scout leader Phoebe Raddings holding a photo of astronaut Bill Anders for all the Cubs to see (also see page 78).

Children from St Peter's Church, Havenstreet, on a Sunday school outing to Alum Bay in 1951. Back row, left to right: Molly George, Audrey Capel, Tom Sivell, Robert Frampton. Second row: John Sivell, Doris George, Joy Hayles (the bear), Pauline Frampton. Third row: Barry Turnball, Michael Corney, Harold George, Susan Eldridge, David Hayles. Front row: Colin Leal, Angela Riddell, Christine Wert, Wendy George, Gillian Leal, Keith Salmon, Margaret Corney, Ruth Wert, Audrey Eldridge, Jacqueline Sivell, Michael Eldridge and his mother Doris.

Brighstone School class 11, 1906. Included are Mr Lempiere (headmaster), Hilda Cooper, Lilian Cooper, Annie Trickett, Dorothy Downer, Annie Cooper, Ethel Downer, Lily Downer, Mabel Dyer and Dorothy Lempiere.

Sister Paul with the infants class of 1953 at St Saviour's Roman Catholic School at Hurst Hill, Totland Bay.

The Island has always been a children's paradise. After the Second World War the children could once again play on the sands. Pictured here in 1948, from left to right, are Hilary White, Peter White and their cousin Gillian Briggs.

Yarmouth Guides and Brownies in the cast of their pantomine 'Mother Goose', which they performed in January 1950. Back row, left to right: Barbara Holloway, Mary Hayles, Margaret Stallard. Second row: Margaret Bradshaw, June Meaning, Delia Hunt, Betty Lock. Third row: Joan Scarf, Shirley Greenen, Thelma Kellaway, Esme Bull, Anne Pitman, Molly Mallett, Effie Pitman, Win Davison, Annette Holloway, Penny Dowden, Vera Archer, Barbara Audis; standing alone at the extreme left is Barbara Saunders. Front row: Sue Hayles, Pat Petitt, Vera Buckley, Diana Ryall, Jenny Cotton, Ann Miles, Mary Stallard, Bridget Hewson, Anne Doe, Camile Harris, Sue Ridett, Sandra Davison. Standing in front of the stage are 'Mac' Donald (left) and Mrs Hans-Hamilton. The goose was played by Serena Hunt.

1st Yarmouth Brownies, 1964. Back row, left to right: Effie Pitman, Lyn Doe, Karen Wellbeloved, Lyn Ketteridge, Mrs Hans-Hamilton, Sherry Fletcher, Sue Cramp, Jenny Stewart, Sandra Davison, Sally Hayles. Front row: Penny Bryant, Jane Cramp, Jane Mallett, Pam Cronin, Dawn Haward, Sarah Foster, Mary Cronin, Vanessa Crismas. Seated at the front is Sue Coombs.

Freshwater Guides on an open night, 6 March 1976. The girls are being taught to light a fire in the old-fashioned way – much to the delight of the audience.

Queen Elizabeth visited Yarmouth on 27 July 1965. Here, Guides, Brownies, Scouts and Cubs form a guard of honour for her at the entrance to Yarmouth Castle.

The Queen enjoying her tour of the castle.

1st Newbridge Cubs on the presentation of a photograph of Bill Anders, one of the Apollo 7 astronauts. This was sent in response to a letter of good wishes sent by the Cub Troop.

Members of the 1st Brighstone Sea Scouts in 1974. The four Venture Scouts pictured here qualified for the coveted Queen's Scout badge. With them is Graeme Dillon, the round-the-world yachtsman, who presented them with their badge certificates. Left to right: Graham Snow, Stephen Parry, Graeme Dillon, Adrian Brook, John Long.

This certificate was presented to patrol leader Ernie Cooper in 1913. It was awarded for his bravery in putting his own life at risk by chasing a pair of bolting horses and eventually bringing them under control, thus saving a number of children in the path of the horses from serious injury or even worse! Ernie remained with the Scouts, holding the position of Scout Master. In 1964 he passed his certificate to his troop to be held in their care.

Two photographs of the same Scouts and Scout Master of the first Brighstone Scout troop in 1911 and 1912. Back row, left to right: Ernest Cooper, Jack Beecham, Fred Frampton, Fred Baker, Alfred Harrison, William Cooper, Alfred Wavell. Middle row: George Cooper, Roland Downer, Eddie Bridges, John Mondrell, Reg Wavell. Front row: Alfred Hams, Bob Frampton, Albert Warne, Martin Edwards, Harry Cogger.

The 1st Brighstone Sea Scout troop have taken part in many combined jamborees over the years. This picture shows the centenary jubilee jamboree in 1957. Included are Messrs Monk, Field Westmore, Salter, Saville, Rushley, Forrester, Davies, Lane, Farrell, Johnson, Whittington, Bravery, Woodford, Bob Downer, Squibbs, Kindersley, Snow, Terry, Sleight, Thomson, Hindmarsh, Harrison, Van Orden, Ware, and Anne Downer.

The 1st Brighstone Baden Powell Scout troop, July 1921. Back row, left to right: R. Shotter, S. Higgins, E. Cooper (Scout Master), J.B. Whitewood, (Asst. Scout Master), L. Hookey. Second row: F. Driver, A. Phillips, W. Shotter, B. Craven. Front row: R. Bendal, F. Harding, G. Orchard, B. Whitehouse.

These seven members of the 1st Brighstone Sea Scouts obtained their Chief Scouts award in 1974. Left to right: R. Brooks, A. Cotton, M. Bridges, F. Russell, P. Snow, A. Cull, N. Morey.

The Freshwater Rover Scouts manning the first fire tender in Freshwater in 1924.

Pupils of Shalfleet C of E School, pictured with their teacher Harry Lock, in 1919. Back row, left to right: Len Saunders, 'Walt' Reynolds, George Baker, Carrie Hodges, Amina Smith, Kath Ray, Alice Baker. Second row: Charlie Ballard, 'Ossie' Cox, 'Boy' Rashley, Nancy Hodges, Albert Taylor, Alf Hayle. Third row: Rita Sheaf, Dorothy Willes, Rene Hendy, Joyce Chiverton, Vera Brett, Eleanor Chambers, Grace Hodges, Winnie Drayton. Fourth row: Alf Jupe, Percy Mussell, Stan Ray, Marjorie Smith, Lydia Hunt, Edith Baker, Stan Willstead, 'Mousey' Brett. Front row: Ron Saunders, Reg Morris, Bert Morris.

Pupils of Brighstone School with Miss Willoughby, the music teacher, after they had won first prize in the Isle of Wight music festival in 1931. Included are N. Harris, J. McIntosh, B. Chessell, R. Whillier, R. Chisholm, L. Harris, H. Buckett, H. King, J. Chisholm, D. Warne, M. Warne, D. Coombe, T. Buckett, C. Cooper, E. Harris, B. Cooper, J. Newbery, B. Cooper and E. Trickett.

Pupils of St Saviour's RC School, Hurst Hill, Totland Bay in 1934. Back row, left to right: Miss Toomey (teacher), Eileen Hood, Peggy Urey, Dolores Newman, Dorothy Smith, Joan Condon, Patsy Newman. Second row: Agnes Timmins, Cissy Burford, Cissy Woodford, Kevin Newman, Peter Cooney, Herbert Hall, Tony Reason, Raymond Millmore, Anges Joynor, May Dimmick, -?-. Third row: George Joynor, Richard Buckett, Rosie Hills, Paul Cooke, Cissy Whitewood, Patrick Breslin, John O Nell. Front row: Lionel Harding, Dennis Gould, -?-, Ronnie B. Nell, Patrick Pryor.

Pupils of St Saviour's RC School, *c.* 1940. Back row, left to right: Dorothy Cooney, Sheila Newman, Agnes Fylan, Nellie Chitty, Doris Smith, Iris Millmore. Second row: Roy Blute, Kevin Newman, Reg Dimmick, Herbert Hall, Robert Taylor, Eric Beeney, Roy Beeney, William Smith, Jerry Jackson, Peter Childs. Third row: Sheila Timmins, Connie Condon, Muriel Breswin, Marjory Beeney, Betty Taylor. Front row: George Franklin, Charles Henry Croad, Arthur Budden, Arthur Fyland, Reg Croad.

Pupils of Brighstone School in 1931. Included are Muriel Snow, Vera Whitewood, Vera Cotton, Alan Cooper, Alice Cotton, Marjorie Chessell, Rose Snow, Ethel Orchard, Winifred Hiskins, Evelyn Barton, Bob Cotton, Fred Harding, Bert Witewood, Bert Whitewood, Bob Cotton II, Gilbert Orchard, Bob Cullen, Mildred Whitwood, Mary Barton, Reg Shotter, Iris Tharle and Edith Cotton.

Pupils from the early days of St Saviour's RC School, proudly posing for their school photograph in 1903. Included are Miss O'Meara, Miss Cokes and Maggie Gould, E. Joynor, P. Urey, H. Hills and R. Whiting.

Brighstone School nativity play, December 1933. Included are Teddy Buckett, Joan Shirley, Cathie Cooper, Joyce Denham, Roy Bridges, George Kimber, Cecil Manner, Raymond Jenning,. Elsie Trickett, Effie Buckett, Jamie Munt, Norah Denham, Mollie Newbery, Lily Munt and Bettey Cooper.

Pupils of the Clifford School of Dance giving a performance in September 1950 at Freshwater memorial hall. The children include J. Bunker, S. Skippins, K. Walsh, H. White, B. Barrett, B. Lee, M. Lyons, J. Lyons, C. Attrill, G. Runyard. David Steele, Pat Clifford and (standing on the piano) Maureen White.

Havenstreet schoolchildren on a day out at Farringford House, Freshwater, *c.* 1930.

Freshwater and Totland Carnival, September 1953. Once again Totland Red Cross win first prize with their tableau called 'The Elizabethans'. Included are Ivy Woodford, Joyce Burford and Beryl Whitewood.

TRANSPORT

*The 12a bus to Totland Bay and Freshwater waits in
Yarmouth Square. Two of the crew are believed to be
Mr Stone and Mr Sivier.*

Before the improvements were made to the Yarmouth ferry terminal in the early 1980s, disembarking and boarding the ferry by foot could be a rather hazardous occupation, as this 1956 photograph shows. But then, in those days, people were deemed more important than cars.

Yarmouth Quay in the 1960s. The slipway has yet to be improved and the larger car ferries have not yet been introduced.

Freshwater, the terminus of the Freshwater to Newport line, was well patronized during the summer months with visitors wishing to see the famous coloured sands of Alum Bay. The 'tourist train', which ran almost non-stop from Ventnor every day, was an extremely popular innovation, and the platform was eventually lengthened to accommodate the summer traffic. The service ceased on 21 September 1953.

A Mew Langton dray delivering to the Crown Inn at Shorwell in 1932.

It took only a light covering of snow on the Broadway, Totland, in 1953 to bring disaster to this Southern Vectis bus. Luckily no one suffered any serious injury when it overturned.

A smiling Mr Burford stands by his Model T Ford in the 1920s. Before 1914 Orchard Bros, grocers of Freshwater Bay, used horse-drawn transport for their deliveries, but when their horses were commandeered for war service they purchased this Model T. Perhaps that's why Mr Burford is smiling.

Yarmouth station, 21 September 1953. The Beeching axe was soon to demolish all main railway services on the Island. The old station building is now a youth club.

In July 1913 the Freshwater, Yarmouth & Newport Railway introduced a small four-wheeled petrol railcar with a semi-open body. There was seating for twelve to fifteen people on three cross bench seats with reversible backs; the vehicle could be driven from either end. For its journey to the Island it was partially dismantled and brought to the lines on a cart. Here it is being unloaded from the cart at Carisbrooke under the supervision of Mr D.R. Lamb of the Great Central Railway. With the advent of Southern Railway this Drewry Car (as it was known) was transferred to their service dock as inspection car no. 437S. It is believed to have been broken up at Newport in 1927.

The Royal Mail coach at the junction of Southdown Road and Afton Road, on its way to Newport via Brook and Shorwell in 1908.

Harry Cooper with guard Bob Sweet, waiting for passengers at Rectory Corner, Freshwater, in 1908. Harry never drove this Royal Mail coach without his dog. The fare to Newport was 7s 6d. A coachman's wage in 1908 was 30s and a guard's 25s per week.

An group leaving the Methodist Church in Avenue Road, Totland, for an outing in 1910. The coach, known to all as the 'Charri', had a seating capacity of twenty, plus driver and guard. The cost of the outing was 7s per person and the total hire of the 'Charri' cost £6.00 for the day.

A church outing in Avenue Road, Totland, in 1919. This is one of Pink's coaches and the driver is Percy Luscombe. The destination was probably Osborne.

Double-decker bus GDL 768E in Yarmouth Square on service 12 to Sandown in 1973. This is believed to have been the last bus to run through the Square and High Street.

Freshwater and Totland Carnival, August 1952. First prize went to the Totland Red Cross float, which depicted their work overseas. Included are Mrs Holland, Miss Meaning, Mrs Whitewood, Mrs Raddings, Miss Woodford, Mrs Hall, Betty and Gwen.

SPORTS & PASTIMES

Members of the URC Women's Guild Committee at a flower festival held at Freshwater United Reformed Church, Guyers Road, in the late 1970s. Left to right: Rene Hannuel, Dorothy Robinson, Doris White (secretary), Dorothy Brignall, Kathleen Geer (chairman), Alice Dimmer (the wife of the minister).

Westover Park (Calbourne) football club, 1930. Back row, left to right: C. Newberry, F. Thomas, B. Hooker, R.F. Weeks, R.G. Green, A.D. Weeks. Front row: J. Hooker, J. Hubbard, W.H. Weeks, R. Harvey, A. Pitman.

Brighstone celebrates the Franz Schubert centenary in 1928. Left to right: Major Blunt, Mrs Street, Mr Roberts, Captain Street; in the centre is ? Street.

THE I. W. FOX HOUNDS MEET AT BRIGHSTONE. NOV. 29. 1907.

As did so many villages in the early years of the century, Brighstone boasted a thriving hunt. Here, the Isle of Wight foxhounds meet at Brighstone on a winter morning in November 1907.

Another pastime was shooting. This is the Rifle Club, probably photographed in the early 1920s.

A concert party was held in Ventnor in 1953 to mark the coronation of Queen Elizabeth II. Here Ernest White (with microphone) leads the singing. Left to right: Barbara Lee, Dorothy Leeson-Towner, David Steele, Peter White, Hilary White, Harry Vickery.

West Wight football club, 1951/2 season. Back row, left to right: H. Read, B. Groves, R. Gregory, ? Maitland, ? Gregory, ? Evans, ? Clarke, H.R. Read, ? Woodford, ? Thompson, ? Beecham. Front row: ? Raish, ? Carter, ? Oliver, ? Hughes, ? Groves.

Brighstone cricket club, 1931. Back row, left to right: K. King, P. Barnes, J. Fisk, J. Orchard, A. Buckett, R. Buckett, F. Cooper (umpire). Front row: R. Chessil, B. Phillips, H. Barnes, R. Downer, H. Cooper.

West Wight football club, Western Divisional Champions 1932/3.

On Saturday 16 July 1910 Robert Loraine was taking part in the Bournemouth flying meeting. The weather was very windy with heavy showers. At about 3 p.m. Loraine decided to take off in the hope of achieving third prize in one of the first aviation races in the South. It was not until 4.30 p.m. that the race officials received a telegram, sent by those manning the Needles light, and later a telephone message, to say that Loraine had landed safely on the downs at Alum Bay. Mr Gallop of Freshwater is believed to have taken these two photographs.

THE WAR EFFORT

Cliff End Fort and Fort Albert Garrison, June 1916.

Brighstone Home Guard, 1945. Back row, left to right: W. Sheath, J. Higgins, A. Sivier, B. Westmore, H. Cassell, F. Hollis, G. Mariner, L. Attrill, C. Newbery, R. Cassell, C. Sivier. Second row: A. Emmett, C. Bullock, B. Phillips, B. Craven, A. Kitson, L. Hookey. Third row: R. Buckett, M. Cotton, C. Bennett, G. Humber, C. Linnington, S. Mew, J. Whitewood, D. Carpenter, H. Brown, S. Hendy. Front row: S. Isaacs, F. Driver, F. Taylor, S. Orchard, W. Emmett, R. Downer.

The Sergeants' Mess of 530 Coastal Regiment RA at the New Needles Battery, 1941. Back row, left to right: Bdr Grimes, -?-, L/Sgt Williams, L/Sgt Davies, Bdr Richardson, L/Sgt Waring, L/Sgt Snellgrove. Second row: Sgt Chandler, Bty Sgt-Maj. C. Blee, Bty Sgt-Maj. J. Dorman, Sgt. S. Coor. Seated at the front are L/Sgt Cram (left) and L/Sgt Rewbridge.

A memento of the First World War – this is the Brooke, Brighstone and Shorwell detachment of the Isle of Wight Volunteer Regiment, 1917. Back row, left to right: Alf Salter, Frank Cotton, F. Harding, George Snow, Ted Scovell, Vic Death, 'Dolf' Downer, Herbert Dore, F. Linnington, Phil Jacobs, William Pragnell, Harry Trickett, Arthur Tharle. Second row: Jack Harding, 'Art' Jones, Fred New, Reg Shirley, -?-, Frank Coleman, 'Walt' Cotton, Bob Buckett, Dave Hookey, Walter Brown, Hilton Snow, Charles Munt, 'Bern' Phillips, Henry Brown. Third row: Fred Ridett, George Cox, Ted Downer, F. Ridett, ? Taylor, Harry Bridges, Jack Creeth, Joe Watson, Walter Jackman, George Morris, Joe Morris, Bert Dyer, Tom Millmore, Arthur Buckett. Front row: Charles Weeks, Jim Woodrow, George Cotton, Percy Foster, 'Bern' Newnham, Arthur Wheeler, A.A.H. Wykeham, 'Perce' Lacey, Walter Heal, Fred Marsh, Will Ridett, M. Calvert.

Many young men from the Isle of Wight served in the trenches in the First World War. These are
volunteers of the Isle of Wight Rifles, probably photographed just before their embarkation for France.

126 New Needles Battery, 530 Coastal Regiment RA, November 1943. Back row, left to right: Gnr Staines, Gnr Davies, Gnr Able, Bdr Cocks, Bdr Arnold, Bdr S. Kin, Gnr Hodgkiss, Gnr Milligan, Gnr Hatcher, Gnr Lickett, L/Bdr Beckerleggs, Gnr Avery, Gnr G. Watson, Gnr Haley, Bdr Easey. Second row: Gnr Smitherman, L/Bdr Guy, Bdr Epps, Gnr Gray, Gnr Williams, Gnr Rees, Gnr Meredith, Gnr Salter, Gnr L. King, Gnr Eyre, Gnr Osborne, Gnr Murche, Gnr Coates, Cpl Sloper. Third row: Gnr W. Wood, Gnr W. Smith, L/Bdr Marshall, L/Bdr Leicester, Gnr Carter, Gnr Draper, Gnr Simms, L/Bdr Harding, Gnr Crews, Gnr Ball, Gnr Harris, Gnr James. Fourth row: L/Sgt Prewett, M/G Muir, Bty Sgt-Maj. Chandler, Lt Mines, Capt. Morton, Lt Lester, Bty Sgt-Maj. Cram, Sgt Rewbridge, L/Sgt Yorke, L/Sgt Orchard. Front row: Gnr N.W. Wood, L/Bdr Baslow, Bdr Snelgrove, Gnr Wright, Gnr Beddow, Gnr Spull, Gnr Cotton, Gnr Harvey, Gnr Woodford, Gnr Bush, Cpl Harradine, Gnr Harvey, Gnr T. Watson. The dog was called Rollo.

The tunnelled entrance to Golden Hill Fort, Freshwater.

Two 4.3 in smooth-bore, barrel-loading guns at Golden Hill fort, in Golden Hill country park. The guns were salvaged from the beach at Fort Albert, Totland, and moved to the fort to help create a decorative entrance, but owing to vandalism and subsequently children climbing on to them and falling, it was decided that they should be removed. The fort itself was built to a hexagonal design between 1863 and 1867 and was to become the hub of the West Wight defence system. It had positions for eighteen guns but they were not all mounted. There was accommodation for 8 officers and 124 men, and hospital facilities for 14 sick or wounded. The fort served as the school of gunnery from 1888 until the Second World War when it was used as a barracks. After the war it was abandoned.

This test-site, near the new Needles Battery, was used by the renowned Saunders Roe company in the mid-1950s for testing the Black Knight rocket, which formed part of the Blue Streak missile. Here a Black Knight rocket is being prepared on the launching pad.

A Black Knight rocket outside the preparation room.

Based at the Needles, 530 Coastal Regiment RA was equipped with 9.2 in guns for coastal defence. The preparation of the shells before firing took place below ground. Armour-piercing shells were used during daylight and high explosive shells at night.

One of the coastal defence 9.2 in guns at the Needles Battery in operation in 1941. The breach is open and the shell tray slung into position to receive the shell from the hoist.

Members of the 530 Coastal Regiment loading a gun at the Needles Battery before a test firing.

The 9.2 in gun in operation. Above: the rangefinder in the battery observation post at the Needles in 1941 being operated by L/Bdr F. Taylor. Below: this information was passed to the gun crews to assist them in laying the gun.

THE CRUEL SEA

A practice launch of the lifeboat Robert Flemming, *1916. Pictured are 'Brandy' Hall and Ernest Edward Conway.*

The Greek ship *Vanvassi* ran aground on the Needles Ledge on 2 January 1947. All her crew were saved by the Yarmouth lifeboat. Included in her cargo were four cows which unfortunately perished, but happily the ship's cat, 'Buddy' (below), was saved, and never put to sea again. He spent his remaining years ashore as the guest of Mrs Attrill of Alum Bay.

The wreck of HMS *Gladiator* after colliding with the SS *St Paul*, an American liner, on 25 April 1908. Captain Lumsden of *Gladiator* managed to beach his stricken vessel at Yarmouth and only twenty-seven lives were lost. She was eventually salvaged and sold for scrap.

This three-masted sailing ship, *The Irex*, ran aground at Scratchells Bay during a heavy storm on 26 January 1890. During this tragic accident three men lost their lives.

After running aground, *The Irex* was battered by heavy seas and eventually broke up.

The wreck of the schooner *Prim,* which ran aground at Atherfield Ledge on 23 February 1912. The heavy seas demasted the *Prim*; one of the masts struck the captain on the head as it fell and killed him. The rest of the crew managed to reach the beach where they stayed till the next morning.

The funeral of the *Prim*'s captain at Brighstone Church on 27 February 1912 (see page 65).

The Briton went aground at Sudmore, Chilton Chine, on 9 January 1906. There was no loss of life and she was later refloated.

The three elder Conway brothers, William (left), George (centre) and Charles, owned the sailing coaster *The Brothers* in which they transported stone from Portland to Totland Beach where it was cut and assembled for the construction of the Needles lighthouse.

Unloading stores for the Needles lighthouse was always risky but the skill of the keepers makes it look easy. They say that the art is always to move on the crest of a wave. But even then a box sometimes nearly gets away, as can be seen below. With the advent of automation at the Needles lighhouse, the keepers have moved to other lighthouses around Britain's coast. The late Revd Freddie Ralph, chaplain to the Needles lighthouse, is featured on the extreme right in both pictures.

The Revd Freddie Ralph, vicar of Christ Church, Totland, and the Revd Mr Land, rector of St James's, Yarmouth, visit the Needles lighthouse, at Christmas 1965. Left to right: Revd Freddie Ralph, Asst Keeper Frank Vaisey, Principal keeper A.T. Whiston, Revd Mr Lang, Asst Keeper Brian Quigley.

Models collected by Ernest Edward Conway. The lifeboat (centre) was presented by Bill Conway to Totland parish council in 1987. It was constructed in 1930 by Lt Cmdr T. Goodman.

Totland Bay lifeboat, the *Robert Flemming*, pictured with her crew in 1924. Left to right: Archie Reed, Tom Cotton, Ernest Conway, George Sanders, Jack Crouch, Charles Conway (coxswain), Frank Gallop (2nd coxswain), 'Dibby' Stallard, Frank Hall, Jessie Kissick, Walt Johnson. Seated are Joss Pragnell and Percy Dory, and in the background is John Page. The *Robert Flemming* was in operation for twenty-three years and rescued thirty people. Charles Conway served for five years as coxswain and for six years as 2nd coxswain.

At one time the beach at Atherfield was one of the best beaches for landing mackerel. This is the crew of a mackerel boat at Atherfield in about 1903.

In the days before the powered lifeboat, small coastal craft acted as lifeboats, often manned by local fishermen and others who devoted their lives to or earned their living from the sea. Their names were often not recorded. This is the Yarmouth boat setting out in the early part of this century. They may have no names but they were truly unsung heroes.

The christening ceremony of the *Joe Jarman* lifeboat in Brighstone in 1893. Her crew consisted of James Cotton (coxswain), Robert Buckett (2nd coxswain), Frank Symonds, Frank Buckett, George Salter jnr, William Merwood, William Holbrook, Walter Cotton, Victor Cotton, Fred Cotton, Robert Buckett jnr, George Salter snr and Charles Holbrook.

Above: the *Worcester Cadet* at Southampton on 19 August 1880, ready to be brought to the Island to take up station at Brighstone Grange. Below: this lifeboat served Brighstone from 11 August 1880 to 17 October 1892 and during this period more than 112 lives were saved. The cost of the lifeboat was defrayed from the *Worcester Cadet* lifeboat fund which was raised by the exertions of Captain J.H. Smith, the former Caption Superintendent of the training ship *Worcester*, stationed at Greenhithe, Kent. In boat, from left to right: Thomas Cotton, Moses Munt (coxswain) N. New, James Cotton, R. Salter, H. Cotton, D. Cotton, J. Gatterall, J. Munt, F. Buckett, J. Cotton, G. Downer, R. Buckett. Standing: James Buckett (ex-coxswain), Revd W.E. Heygate (rector), George Wyatt (hon. treasurer from 1859), George Tubbs (Coastguard officer). Some years later, on 9 March 1888, the coxswain Moses Munt and 2nd coxswain Tom Cotton were to lose their lives while attempting a rescue on the SV *Sirenia*.

The *Susan Ashley* was the Brook lifeboat from 3 September 1907 to 31 March 1937. She was the last and the longest serving of all the Brighstone Bay lifeboats. At the end of her service she was sold to Mr Hescroft of Poole who converted her into a yacht and renamed her *Susan of Poole*. She was seen visiting Yarmouth in 1957 and as late as 1987 appeared in the film of Erskine Childers' famous thriller *The Riddle of the Sands*.

Lord Mottistone at a practice launch of the Brook lifeboat, *Susan Ashley*. He was part of the lifeboat crew for many years and was elected as coxswain, a position which he bravely carried out until leaving for war service in 1915 when Ben Jacobs took his place. During a rescue attempt on 21 October 1891 Lord Mottistone, when the lifeboat was struggling to get alongside a stricken vessel, dived into the water and swam to the sinking craft, thus enabling the rescue to proceed, and saving the lives of those on board.

The Brighstone lifeboat *The Brothers Brickwood* ready for sea trials with tipping plates in position. The crew consisted of James Cotton (coxswain), Robert Buckett (2nd coxswain), ? Bowman, Frank Edmunds, Walter Cotton, Charles Holbrook, William Holbrook, George Shotter, Frank Buckett, Robert Buckett jnr, John Creeth, Edwin Munt and Aaron Downer. *The Brothers Brickwood* served at Brighstone Grange from 1907 to 1915 when the station finally closed. After her withdrawal from service in 1915, she was placed on the RNLI reserve list. In 1918 she was called to the Scarborough station where she served until 1924 when she was sold to the Latvian Life Saving Society for £150.

The crew of the new lifeboat, *The Brothers Brickwood*, at Brighstone Grange in 1903.

ACKNOWLEDGEMENTS

As with all the volumes in this series, this book would not have been possible but for the generosity and assistance of so many good people. I would therefore like to thank the following:

Edith Baker and her sister of Newbridge; Sue Bird, Yarmouth Girl Guides; Bill Blackmore, Totland historian and original archivist; Brighstone Reading Rooms; Brighstone Scouts; Bob Buckett, builder of Brighstone; Bill Conway of Colwell Bay; Geoff Cotton of Yarmouth; Bert Draper of Newport; Revd T. Eady, rector of Brighstone; Farringford Hotel; The Fire Brigade, Newport (Operational Support Section); Heather Freeman of Stone Close, Ningwood; John Honeychurch, Totland parish hall committee; Malcolm Johnson, Southern Vectis; Dave Kennet of Mill Road Garage, Yarmouth, and recently retired coxswain of the Yarmouth lifeboat; Colin Leal of Havenstreet; Fr Clemment-Marshall, priest, St Saviour's RC Church, Totland Bay; The Lord Mottistone; North Court House, Shorwell; Lt Cmdr Tom Peppitt RNR; Wayne Pritchett, Newport harbourmaster; Phoebe Raddings, Hon. Commissioner IOW Cub Scouts; St Saviour's RC School, Totland Bay; Audrey Smith, archivist, Totland parish council; Les Turner of Yarmouth; Keith and Alan Weeks of Calbourne Water Mill; and The West Wight Football Club.

May I especially thank my friend and colleague Peter T.G. White for all his help in the preparation of this book, and finally, my wife Melodina for her extreme patience and constant supplies of refreshment when we have been 'burning the midnight oil'.